Growing Through Loss

A Handbook for Grief Support Groups

D1616254

Jean Monbourquette

Growing Through Loss

A Handbook for Grief Support Groups

NOVALIS

Growing Through Loss:
A Handbook for Grief Support Groups
is published by Novalis
as part of the *Life in Christian Community* series.

Translation of: *Groupe d'entraide pour personnes en deuil: Comment l'organiser et le diriger*

Translation: Brigitte Caron

Cover and layout: Gilles Lépine

© 1994, Novalis, St. Paul University, Ottawa, Canada

Business Office: Novalis, 49 Front St. East, 2nd Floor, Toronto, Ontario, M5E 1B3

Editorial Office: Novalis, 223 Main Street, Ottawa, Ontario, K1S 1C4

Legal deposit: 2nd trimester, 1994
    National Library of Canada
    Bibliothèque nationale du Québec

Printed in Canada

Canadian Cataloguing in Publication Data

Monbourquette, Jean

    Growing through loss: A handbook for grief support groups
Includes bibliographical references.

ISBN 2-89088-672-7

    1. Bereavement—Psychological aspects.
2. Counselling—Handbooks, manuals, etc.   I. Title

BF575.G7M65313 1994   155.9'37   C94-900452-9

NOVALIS

Contents

Introduction

*Why form support groups
for people who are experiencing grief?*

There are very few social rituals to help us come to terms with grief. This cultural denial of death and suffering can have damaging effects on individuals and on communities that are experiencing a loss. Eventually the importance of grieving as a process of healing is forgotten, and healthy ways to grieve are lost.

At the request of many counsellors, I have decided to share my knowledge and experience of support groups for the bereaved. Many "people-helpers" have realized how crucial it is that individuals come to terms with their grief to maintain their physical, mental and spiritual health. By forming grief support groups, they want to give those who grieve an opportunity to share their pain with others. In this way they hope to prevent the many psychological and social problems that are common among people, families and communities who do not have the support they need to mourn the inevitable losses of life.

For whom is this guide intended?

I have had many people in mind while writing this book: psychologists, pastoral counsellors, social workers, volunteers working in palliative care units, and counsellors working in funeral parlours with bereaved families. I have also thought of non-professionals who have the skills and knowledge necessary to lead a group of people who are experiencing a loss.

I sincerely hope that this simple and practical guide will help all of you give support to persons who are going through the process of grief.

Chapter One:

How support groups work

The organization of a support group

The leader's role

Suggestions and guidelines for participants

The support group's creed

A meeting outline

Suggestions for moments of silence or prayer

Organization of a support group

A support group is made up of people who have met with a similar sorrow and who want to be healed through the process of sharing their experiences and knowledge of healing. It is sometimes called a self-help group or a sharing group.

A support group is different from a therapeutic group in that it is set up by non-professionals. The participants are not clients and there are no fees. If a health professional is leading the group, it is to receive help himself or herself, or to train future leaders.

This type of spontaneous group, made up of people facing a common challenge, needs no official authorization because it does not pretend to give professional help. The group simply provides support and help, even if professionals act as supervisors or resource people.

One requirement for the success of the group: Homogeneity

Support groups will be most effective if they are made up largely of people who share a similar experience (such as the death of a child, a parent or a spouse), or who are in the same age group (children, teenagers, adults).

Some types of loss may require a specialized group. In the case of suicide, for example, it is vital to dwell on certain aspects of grief and to deal with feelings of guilt in depth. If it is not possible to form a homogeneous group, a group with people who have suffered different kinds of loss will still be very helpful.

Note, however, that combining bereaved and divorced people is not recommended. These two types of loss are very different: a person who has lost someone to death has not really experienced a failed relationship.

Publicizing your group

There are many ways to make the existence of your support group known:

- word of mouth and personal contacts;
- referrals from professionals, including priests, physicians, social workers and nursing staff;
- referrals from social agencies: community health or social centres, schools, parishes, hospitals and funeral parlours;
- press releases on the community television channel, on the radio, in social events calendars and in the local newspaper;
- information brochures placed in professionals' waiting rooms, community centres, social agencies, hospitals, funeral parlours, church notice boards and convenience stores.

Meeting place

A public place should be chosen, rather than a private home. It should be accessible to public transportation. It should be quiet, and the chairs should be comfortable. Any rental fees should be covered by the participants.

Frequency and length of meetings

Meetings should take place at least once a week and last no longer than two hours. A series of 12 meetings should allow profound healing to take place. An excellent way to accelerate one's mourning period and to give support to new participants is to take part in a second and perhaps even a third series of 12 meetings.

Number of participants

Ideally a group should be composed of 7 to 10 persons. However it can have as few as 5 and as many as 12. In cases where there are more than 12 people it is better to form two smaller groups.

New members can join a group after the first meeting has taken place, but this is not possible after the second meeting. The addition of new members would interfere with the journey together in which members were engaged.

Selection of members

Careful selection of the participants is important. Some people need special attention: persons who are having psychological problems, such as those who threaten suicide or who ramble on, or who are unable to follow a conversation, or those who are under the influence of drugs or alcohol. You should refer them to professional services. Putting members of the same family in a group is not advisable. Often they will be hesitant to open up for fear of hurting a sibling, a parent or a child. Sometimes, however, it may be beneficial for a couple to be in the same group.

A tool: The personal journal

We strongly advise participants to continue the work that they start in each meeting afterwards at home. This can take the form of a journal or of tape recordings. The person can write or tape thoughts and reflections, make a note of tasks to be done, and record his or her progress. Also the individual can note titles of books that may be helpful to read after the meetings have ended.

The journal entries or tape recordings are strictly confidential. The participants will never have to read passages from the journal during meetings. On the other hand, those who wish may do so freely.

The leader's role

An effective leader must:

- have experienced his or her own grief and have overcome it, at least partially;
- be able to assume responsibility for a group, and have enough time to do so;
- be able to create an atmosphere of comfort, safety and open communication;
- be sensitive to other people's feelings and understand the importance of expressing them;
- be able to share briefly his or her own experience in order to help group members to speak about themselves;
- understand that knowing all the answers is not necessary; encouraging participants to share with one another is most important;
- be comfortable with silence and give others the opportunity to speak about their own experience;
- be able to allow participants to express their pain and anger and to explain that the emotions are appropriate (put a box of tissues in view);
- be patient and respectful, while at the same time limiting the duration of each person's contribution;
- be able to distance oneself from the participants' criticism of the contents of the meetings or the techniques used; (adopt an open and receptive

attitude; the leader has nothing to prove or to defend; ask anyone who criticizes if he or she has suggestions to improve the situation, and invite them to participate in finding a solution);

- be very disciplined about time spent with individual group members; (prolonging the meeting with one or a few participants is not advisable; it is better to refuse any requests for a private meeting, while encouraging the individual to share with the whole group what he or she wants to say);

- be willing to ask for professional supervision for oneself, or for difficult cases requiring professional care.

The leader is responsible for:

- preparing before each meeting physically (rest, relaxation), psychologically (a confident attitude), spiritually (a willingness to serve others);

- planning the tasks assigned to participants: readings, rest periods, and so forth;

- preparing a few open questions, e.g., "How does tonight's topic relate to your experience?"; "How do you feel about tonight's topic?"; "What is important for you in tonight's topic?";

- giving information, if necessary, about the grieving process, its stages and the different ways to handle these stages; and,

- adhering to the meeting's agenda, especially the time for opening and closing.

Suggestions for leaders

- Get to know the participants on a first-name basis as soon as possible, and use their names.

- Avoid prescribing behaviour, such as saying, "You should...," or "You should not...." Give participants useful information—and encourage them to share their own—without giving advice.

- Sum up discussions that seem to drag on. Emphasize the main point and ask participants to give others a chance to express themselves. Let them know that you will come back to them when everyone has had an opportunity to speak.

- Suggest a few books or contact people to invite to a meeting if members express such a need.

Suggestions and guidelines for participants

A support group is more than a gathering of people in the same location. It is an entity. It generates a strength and energy that will affect all its members. And all participants can expect the support that they need from this group in their experience of grief.

In the context of a support group no one is forced to speak. The quiet listeners can find comfort by simply being there. By listening to others they may find a model of emotional expression and be able to share other people's suffering. As such, the group is a privileged learning context.

Guidelines

To meet these objectives the group members must respect some specific guidelines.

- Discretion. Each member must agree to keep confidential what is said and done in the group.

- Respect. If a member decides to leave the group before the completion of the series, he or she must come to the next meeting to say good-bye.

- Attendance. If a member cannot attend a meeting, he or she must notify the leader.

- Perseverance. The members are committed to be there even in difficult times.

- Punctuality. The members must arrive on time and stay until the end.

- Freedom. No one is forced to speak.

- Acceptance. There are no good or bad emotions or questions; everything is acceptable as long as it doesn't involve judging members.

- Sharing. The meeting is organized in a way that allows everyone to express himself or herself. Private conversations are discouraged during the meetings.

- Openness. During the meetings, participants will abstain from smoking or drinking, which can be ways of masking anxiety, and be willing to experience and express their anxiety.

The support group's creed

The following affirmations describe the process of grief through which a bereaved person passes and express its basic principles. It is based on the creed professed by Alcoholics Anonymous (AA) groups. The support group's creed may be read out loud beginning with the third meeting. It helps to strengthen the participants' faith—a faith that may waver at times—in their ability to heal, and helps them recall the beliefs that underlie the process of resolving grief.

1. We believe that losing loved ones is a natural part of life and that it is important to experience grief in order to heal.
2. We believe that grief is not an illness, but a stage of growth which everyone passes through on the way towards greater maturity.
3. We believe that knowing that grieving requires energy and courage is important.
4. We believe that having a place to express suffering without fear of judgement is important.
5. We believe that it is necessary to be listened to and encouraged by others.
6. We believe that real emotions are good, and that they change as soon as they are expressed.
7. We believe that each member must experience the various stages of grief in his or her own way.
8. We believe that we all have the necessary resources to experience grief and come out of it a better and freer person.

A meeting outline

A support group meeting generally follows 8 or 9 steps:

1 *Welcome*

The moment when the leader welcomes each participant individually is very important. It contributes to creating a climate of confidence. It helps relieve fear and resistance, especially during the first meetings. The leader makes himself or herself available during the first few minutes by offering a handshake, making eye-contact, making small talk, and giving practical information (such as the location of the coat room and the rest room).

2 *Centering*

The meeting begins with a moment of silence. It may consist of a relaxation exercise, an appropriate short prayer, an "energy chain" or a brief reading— anything which can help break the hold of extraneous distractions. The aim of centering is to foster inner peace, and to let one truly be present to oneself and to the group. If a member chooses not to take part in this exercise, he or she could leave the room while it is taking place. If the entire group chooses not to do this exercise, it is preferable not to impose it.

3 *Reading of the creed*

The group's creed is the ideological foundation which unites the members of the group. It should be read by a different person each time, if possible. It is an opportunity to stress the objectives and purpose of the meetings.

4 Review of the week

The participants are invited to tell how their week has gone since their last meeting. Those who wish can talk about their experience of grief and their progress through the week. The leader assesses the value of the exchange and may decide that some of the information shared is important enough to spend some time on, perhaps even the entire evening.

5 Introduction of the meeting's theme

The leader introduces the theme or the stage of grief that will be covered during the meeting. (In Chapter 3 there is a list of proposed themes for the 12 meetings.) If the group prefers to focus on a different aspect of grief than the one suggested, it is best to follow the wishes of the majority. In fact, this means that the members of the group are taking responsibility for their healing process.

The leader intervenes only if the members stray to a topic unrelated to their grief. He can ask them if that is what they really want to discuss, while making it clear that they are missing the group's objectives. If the participants clearly decide to avoid talking about grief, the leader has every right to leave.

6 Exchange and sharing

The participants discuss the theme or any other aspect of grief. The leader gives adequate time for each member to speak, fosters the free expression of thoughts and feelings, reformulates these contributions, and invites quieter persons to share, without forcing them. (See "The leader's role" on page 14.)

7 Health break

A different member should be invited to take responsibility for the health break each week. It should be kept simple to avoid competition between members: coffee, juice, cookies. This informal time may foster openness and intimacy.

8 Adjournment of the meeting

This is the time :

- to make announcements, such as birthdays;
- to propose an assignment for the coming week;
- to suggest reading material;
- to inform participants about conferences or workshops on grief;
- to wish participants a week of healing.

9 Prayer or energy chain

Some groups may wish to close with a prayer, such as the AA serenity prayer, or an "energy chain". You will find suggestions on the following pages.

Suggestions for moments of silence or prayer

The Lord's Prayer

The Serenity Prayer

> *Lord, give me the serenity*
> *to accept the things I cannot change,*
> *the courage to change the things I can change,*
> *and the wisdom to know the difference.*

A prayer entitled, "He takes care of us"

> *I am convinced, Lord,*
> *that you always meet us as we are.*
> *You do not abandon us*
> *in our weakness, our suffering or our depression.*
> *You walk with us wherever we go.*
> *You do not turn your back on us*
> *when we are weak, hurt or depressed.*
> *Over the years, with kindness and patience,*
> *you give us the fullness of your grace,*
> *as we are ready to embrace it.*

Elizabeth Dean Bunham

A prayer to a silent God

> *Sometimes, God, I get angry with You,*
> *with the suffering which overwhelms me,*
> *body and soul.*
> *Sometimes, I ask You:*
> *What do You mean by this loss?*
> *What truth do You want to teach me?*

What direction do You want me to take?
I know that You want to reveal something to me.
Sometimes, I get impatient with You
and I feel that You are taking too long
to reveal Your plan to me.

Jean Monbourquette

A prayer to the God of the living

God of the living,
give me the grace and the courage
never to give up or surrender to despair,
neither in the face of life nor in times of death,
neither because of illness nor because of suffering,
nor because of passing discouragements,
even in the face of my own death;
but to transform everything, as your Son Jesus did,
into a gesture of freedom, an act of life,
an offering of love.

Spontaneous prayers

If all of the participants wish, they may offer their own spontaneous prayers at the end of the meeting. These can take on different forms.

- A relational prayer, in which they tell God about their experience on the emotional level.

- An offering to God of their sufferings, and their joys, in union with Christ.

- A prayer of thanksgiving, in which they thank God for the progress they are making.

- A prayer of petition for themselves, their families, or other participants, to help them overcome their difficulties.

Silent prayer or "energy chain"

> This option may be preferable, especially when the members of the group are not Christians.
>
> 1. Take a moment to centre yourself.
> 2. Put on a selection of soothing music.
> 3. End with an "energy chain," inviting participants to join hands and to send each other, in the silence of their hearts, energy to heal and to accept their emotional state.

Chapter Two:

The stages of grief

The reality of grief in the face of a loss
Stages of grief
Brief description

1   Shock
2   Denial
3   Releasing emotions
4   Completing the tasks related to grieving
5   Discovering the meaning of the loss
6   Forgiving
7   Claiming your legacy
8   Acknowledging the end of grief and celebrating it

The reality of grief in the face of a loss

Definition of "grief"

The word "grief" is derived from *gravis*, which means "heavy," as in "gravity." To be afflicted with grief means to be burdened and weighed down.

The word "grief" can have several meanings. Sometimes it presupposes a loss: "He grieves." Sometimes it describes a social state: "She is in mourning." Sometimes it refers to an emotional and psychological process leading to healing: "He is going through the grieving process."

Grief and attachment

To understand the grieving process, one must recognize that human beings are creatures of attachment. Without attachment life is not possible. This is why we build relationships with loved ones and why these relationships become psychological and spiritual bonds. These bonds are characterized by various degrees of intensity. Undoubtedly a "fusional" or symbiotic bond is more intense than a bond of friendship, even if the latter is quite profound.

Generally, people become attached to other people. However, we can become attached to any reality in which we have an emotional investment. By investing affective energy in an object, a place, a pet, a period of our lives, an idea, an activity or a hobby, we develop attachments, charging these things with symbolic significance.

When we lose this person or thing, our attachment system is wounded. Since our organism knows how to protect its integrity and to grieve, it automatically begins the healing process. This process of emotional healing is known as the resolution of grief.

The grieving process

The grieving process is a naturally occurring human response. It is not an illness. Unfortunately, the denial of suffering and death in our society often hinders the natural resolution of grief. Being forced to hide and repress our pain not only causes stress but can even cause sickness.

When people complete all the stages of grief, they are able to resume a normal life and can even be profoundly transformed. They can establish new relationships in a less fusional and more adult way.

Avoiding the grieving process

When it is impossible to experience all the stages of grief, a person who lacks healthy attachments will tend to seek out compensatory ones. These may give him or her the illusion of not having experienced the loss. Unfortunately, a person who has lost someone and is unable to let go may continue to seek a relationship that doesn't exist anymore, instead of establishing new ones.

This avoidance has several causes. Our society lacks social rituals that would aid the grieving process. There is very little information that actually teaches us how to grieve, many of us do not have the ability to fully express our emotions, and so forth.

Grief and life

Grief is the necessary waiting period between two attachments; one that you have left or have lost, and one that will form in the future, which will be different from the previous one.

Although we cannot live without attachments, these are never eternal. They always result in some form of separation. We can see the truth of this from the time of our birth. Life is an uninterrupted sequence of attachments and separations, of deaths and births. We must learn to die to one condition in order to be born to another: this is simply intrinsic to life. Grief is an integral part of living, part of the foundation of life.

The individual and collective meanings of grief

Grief is an individual process as well as a collective one. The entire community mourns the loss of a person who has established many relationships with his or her fellows. For this reason a bereaved person must embrace solidarity with others as well as solitude. The loss of a member of a family, of a community, or of a village affects everyone and reminds each of us of our own losses. When the whole community loses one of its own, all the members are confronted by their own mortality.

Stages of grief

Dr. Elizabeth Kübler-Ross, the American psychiatrist, identified five stages related to dying. Since then we have studied the psychological processes experienced by grieving persons, and have identified seven stages in the grieving process.

The first two stages, shock and denial, are reactions of resistance to the tremendous trauma caused by the loss. They are followed by the release or expression of emotions and feelings, which constitutes a kind of purging of the biological and psychological bonds with the lost one.

Once the emotions are released, the bereaved person undertakes the tasks related to grieving. This means completing in a tangible way, things that remain unfinished.

The next stage is of a more spiritual nature. It consists of discovering the meaning of the loss. This stage is followed by a period of forgiveness: forgiving oneself, forgiving the other person, and asking for forgiveness. At the end of the process comes the legacy, in which the bereaved person can recover all the love and energy that he or she had invested in the lost one. After this phase, the completion of the grieving process is made "official".

These stages are only a rough sketch. As such, they describe the various steps in the healing process. Note that they should never be used to label people: while the sequence described here is the most common one, the stages may occur in a different order and may be accompanied by setbacks. Each person is unique and lives a unique story. Our theories should never limit the reality of a person's experience.

Brief description

1   **Shock**

This stage is characterized by a state of emotional and perceptual paralysis. When people hear tragic news, they become numb and unable to experience the full emotional reaction caused by the loss. They may create fantasies about the lost one. They may hallucinate the presence of the deceased.

They may close off reality even more if they were unable to see, touch or speak to the deceased before the end. For some people the grieving process can only begin when they actually see the body.

2   **Denial**

Denial is another form of resistance to pain. Adults can act like children who believe that they can erase reality by hiding it. Denial is helpful because it delays full consciousness of a tragic event. If the loss were too great, this awareness or consciousness of the tragedy could cause some people to lose their psychological balance.

The first form of denial is cognitive: the person denies the loss, tries to forget it or not to think about it. The second form of denial is emotional. People are unable to express their emotions. They either do not know how to do so, or they are afraid that they will become overwhelmed by them.

Denial can take many forms, such as over-activity, starting another relationship immediately, finding a culprit, idealizing the lost one, using drugs, psychosomatic symptoms, and so on.

Denial is a transitional stage between the occurrence of a loss and the full awareness of that loss. It takes place usually at the beginning of the grieving process and may seem like a form of bargaining. It is a time during which people are torn between separation and attachment. They may imagine ways to bring back the lost one without believing that these could actually work. At the end of the denial/bargaining phase, when they realize that all their dealings have not accomplished anything, they will probably experience deep sadness.

3   Releasing emotions

When people let down their defences and become fully aware of having suffered a loss, many emotions will arise—anxiety, powerlessness, sadness, anger, guilt, and perhaps even a feeling of liberation.

Anxiety and fear

People can feel anxious and afraid when they see their life collapse as a result of a loss. This anxiety stems from a feeling of powerlessness in the face of death. People may feel as if they have lost control of their own life and the lives of their loved ones. At times, this fear is obvious; it wells up when denial and anger have failed to bring back the loved one. Those whose survival depends on others will be very frightened at being separated from a loved one.

Another fear among grieving persons is that their intense emotional state may make them social misfits. "What if my pain turns me into someone different from others? What if I do not fit in anymore?" This reaction is especially common among grieving children. Children may go so far as avoiding their friends for fear of letting their pain show and being rejected because of it. The isolation created by fear allows the person to focus on the memory of the lost loved one and to maintain an internal dialogue with that person. Fear is a survival tool. Its purpose is to keep the lost relationship alive.

Sadness

Sadness is *the* emotion of grief. It is provoked by the first real awareness of a loss. It feels like an inner tearing. In fact, it marks the beginning of a purging period. It is the heart expressing its pain. While going through it, some people may feel overwhelmed, as if they are being crushed by sadness.

Accepting this stage is crucial for healing. Allowing a person to fully embrace this experience, accompanying them, inviting them to talk and letting them weep, are all very important. This sadness may be coupled with bouts of depression, chronic fatigue, short attention span, self-accusation, or insomnia.

Anger

Anger is a spontaneous protest in the face of such a cruel loss. In the midst of this realization, bereaved persons may feel abandoned, even rejected, by their loved one. This may create feelings of anger in them, which they will find difficult to experience, let alone express. Expressing anger, especially towards a deceased one, is not socially acceptable. There may be a temptation to transfer this feeling of anger onto the nursing staff, relatives, or friends. The bereaved one needs to make someone responsible for the death of his or her loved one.

Expressing these feelings of anger is essential, even though people may have difficulty acknowledging their anger towards a loved one who has left them. We must remind them that denying this anger is unfair towards the deceased. In fact, anger is a healthy emotion that can naturally be directed towards loved ones. Anger and love for the same person are not incompatible. On the contrary, we can only feel such deep emotions in a context of profound attachment.

Guilt

To find an answer to their anguish and to maintain inner stability, children tend to scale everything down to their own level. For example, they may feel responsible for the separation of their parents, for the death of their grand-parents and so on. Bereaved people may also turn their anger on themselves and harbour deep feelings of guilt. They may feel that their loved one has died because of their nastiness. They reactivate the magical thinking of the child in them. They want to compensate for the lack of stability by feeling guilty and responsible.

Feelings of liberation

The experience of a loss may be accompanied by feelings of liberation. The parents that we loved dearly may be delivered from their long suffering by death. Their death may mean that we can resume a more normal life after months, even years, spent at a bedside. Inherent to every misfortune is release from the anxiety caused by the threat to a life. The fear of hardship is often greater than the hardship itself, especially when the threat is long-lived. Helping the bereaved person express and appreciate this feeling of relief, without guilt, is very important.

Full awareness of the loss and acceptance

This stage is reached when people stop denying and bargaining and become fully aware of the scope of their loss. At this point, they may feel that they have reached a point of no return. It is the end of their attachment.

This realization is characterized by a sadness so intense that it may reach a level of lamentation. However, this crisis of pain is short-lived. It also leads to a feeling of relief and peace, that the worst is over and that healing can begin.

This painful stage is also the stage of acceptance, when the wound truly begins to heal. The previous stages consisted of cleaning the wound by becoming aware of it, thus creating the conditions needed for healing to begin. The bereaved may then talk about their loss without being overwhelmed by emotions. They will be able to make plans for the future. They accept the loss and the absence in their lives.

This is a pivotal moment. It confirms that grief does *not* mean forgetting the loved one, but instead, that there is a different kind of connection.

4 Completing the tasks related to grieving

Once the emotional work is almost complete, we must undertake the tasks related to grief. These include finishing incomplete dialogues, either orally or through letters, placing the photographs of the deceased in albums, giving away the belongings of the loved one, fulfilling promises made to them, and so on.

5 Discovering the meaning of the loss

This stage involves finding meaning in our experience of loss. All losses are accompanied by a significant gain in maturity. It is an opportunity to discover more about ourselves and others. We can ask ourselves what new resources this situation has elicited from us. It is a time of gifts and benefits. It is the time to transform hardship into gold.

To understand this idea more fully, you might read Victor Frankl's book, *Finding Meaning In Our Lives*.

6 Forgiving

At this stage, most people go through a ritual of forgiveness. Its purpose is to eliminate any lingering feelings of resentment and guilt. When we forgive the one who has left us, we cleanse ourselves of anger. By forgiving ourselves and by asking forgiveness for our own weaknesses and lack of love, we become freed from unhealthy guilt and regain our inner peace. To do this, we must turn often to the wealth of our spiritual life.

7 Claiming your legacy

This is the final stage. Helping someone to experience the ritual of legacy is probably easier than explaining it.

In the course of a relationship, we invest a lot of ourselves in our loved one and develop many expectations. These are projections of ourselves onto the other person's reality. To avoid coming out of grief with the feeling of having been cheated or betrayed, we must, through the ritual of legacy, reclaim all that we have invested in the other. (See the description of the twelfth meeting on the ritual of legacy.)

8 Acknowledging the end of grief and celebrating it

Once the ritual of legacy has been experienced with peace and serenity, it is important to publicly proclaim the end of grief. This announcement by the leader is a form of social permission for the resolution of grief. It allows a person to leave the past behind and to open up to the future with greater maturity.

Chapter Three:

Support groups for grieving persons

Twelve meeting outlines

First meeting: Defining the objectives of the group and of each participant

Second meeting: Telling the story of our grief

Third meeting: Fostering the hope of resolving our grief

Fourth meeting: Coming to terms with our resistance to the loss and expressing our sadness.

Fifth meeting: Becoming aware of our anger and expressing it

Sixth meeting: Expressing our feelings of guilt and letting them be transformed

Seventh meeting: Taking care of ourselves during the grieving process

Eighth meeting: Shedding light on our human relationships

Ninth meeting: Becoming pro-active and resolving unfinished business

Tenth meeting: Discovering a meaning to our loss

Eleventh meeting: Forgiving ourselves and the person we have lost

Twelfth meeting: Claiming our legacy

Defining the objectives of the group and of each participant

The meeting's theme:

> "This is what I lost..., this is what I am hoping for ...."

Objectives

1. To state for whom you are grieving.
2. To describe in what state you would like to be at the end of the twelve meetings.

Meeting outline

1 *Greeting*

The leader will warmly greet each participant.

2 *Information*

The leader, or one of the members, will give necessary information about parking, rest rooms, cloakroom, telephone number at the meeting place, and so on.

3   Introduction of the leader

The leader will welcome the group and introduce himself or herself. He will briefly explain who he is and why he accepted the leadership of this group. He will say a few words about how he perceives his role.

He will acknowledge the courage of the people present and congratulate them for having overcome any fear or inner resistance to sharing their pain. At the same time, he will acknowledge that each person has a part of themselves which is hesitant to express suffering, afraid of increasing the suffering by doing so.

4   Introduction of the participants

This introduction should be simple and brief. Participants will state their name, their occupation, and how they found out about this group. Make sure that people do not begin talking about their pain right away. They can do so after step 5.

5   Introduction of the guidelines

The leader will emphasize the importance of the group in the grieving process and will introduce the procedural guidelines. Make sure that everyone understands them well and agrees to follow them. (See "Suggestions and guidelines for participants" on page 17.)

6   Introduction of the participants' grief

The members will now be invited to share their grief. At this point the leader will only ask questions which may help each person feel more comfortable. He will make notes of each person's statements.

7 Defining individual objectives

The participants are invited to write on a piece of paper what they expect from these meetings and to describe the emotional state they would like to have by the end. The leader will also record these statements.

Questions that could help the participants express themselves include:

"What do you expect from this meeting?";

"In what state do you want to be at the end of the twelve meetings?"

The leader must ensure that the objectives are stated positively and in very clear detail: for example, "I would like to stop repressing"; "What do you want to stop repressing? Can you state that positively?" The leader may point out that the simple process of creating specific goals means that the individual is ready at the level of the unconscious to realize them.

8 Summary of the objectives

The leader will collect the statement of objectives of each member without making any judgements or promises. With this information he should be able to define the objectives of the group as a whole.

9 Health break

10 Adjournment of the meeting

Make a brief assessment to determine what could be improved. Pass out a sheet of paper on which the members can write their names, addresses and phone numbers. Suggest that the participants acquire a note book.

11 Prayer or moment of silence

See "Suggestions for moments of silence or prayer" on page 23.

Elements to look for:

It is important to make sure that everyone has the opportunity to express themselves, while stressing that anyone is free to refrain. The time allotted to each member must not be too long; their story of grief can wait until the next meeting. Going too deeply into the emotional realm at this point is not advisable. Too much emotion right away may frighten off some members whose trust in the value of the group may still be uncertain.

To know if you have met the objectives of the meeting, ask yourself the following questions.

(Answer these questions alone or with your supervisor.)

How have you, as leader of the group, experienced the meeting?

Are there aspects you would like to modify?

Have people left feeling reassured and confident?

Has each person had a chance to express themselves?

Are you aware of anyone who should be referred to a professional?

Some helpful readings from *To Love Again* (Jean Monbourquette, 1993):

You belong to the community of the suffering, p. 64;

Must you be born to death as you are to life? p. 122.

Second meeting

Telling the story of our grief

The meeting's theme:

"The pain of my own story."

Objectives

1. To tell the story of our grief.
2. To re-live the pain caused by the loss, in a supportive environment.

Meeting outline

1   Greeting and opening remarks

2   Introduction of newcomers by the leader

Newcomers then tell the group their occupation and how they heard about the group. The participants from the first meeting briefly introduce themselves to those who are new.

For the first few meetings, wearing name tags may be helpful. The leader can pass out a list of names and ask the newcomers to put their names on it.

3   Review of the group's guidelines

The leader will review the guidelines agreed upon by the members at the previous meeting. The leader will explain these guidelines to the newcomers.

4   A word from the newcomers

Upon being invited by the leader, the newcomers will tell the others:

- for whom they are grieving; and
- their objectives in joining this group.

(The participants from the first meeting do not have to repeat this part.)

5   Objectives

The leader will present a brief review of the group's objectives.

6   The meeting's theme

The leader will present the theme for the evening and invite each person to recount, in detail, the story of their own loss.

The leader can use the following questions to elicit the telling of each story:

"When did you find out that X was dying?"

"Who informed you of the death?"

"What did you experience at that moment?"

"Would you have liked to say more to X before he or she died?"

If participants express themselves easily there is no need to interrupt them. If they start weeping, tell them that this is the place to do it. Place a box of tissues in plain view to give them permission to cry.

If some participants are overcome by emotion to the point of being unable to speak, remind them to take their time and to breathe through their pain. Invite another participant to hold their hand during painful moments. Make sure, however, that these gestures of comfort are appropriate.

Through the telling of their story, it may be possible to discover who in the person's family or circle of friends may have said or done something that caused the person to become emotionally closed off.

If some participants are unable to tell their story because of a lack of time, tell them that they will be the first to speak at the next meeting.

7 Health break

8 Adjournment of the meeting

It is common for members of such a group to develop bonds with each other and to support one another very effectively between meetings. You could suggest a phone support line to those who are interested.

Pass out the list of names and ask members who would be interested in receiving calls from others to put an X next to their name.

Circulate the list one more time so that each person can see who is and who is not interested.

Point out that phone conversations of 20 minutes or less are advisable.

Mention the value of a journal and invite members to record in it the highlights of their story.

9 *Prayer or moment of silence*

See "Suggestions for moments of silence or prayer" on page 23.

To know if you have met the objectives of the meeting, ask yourself the following questions.

(Answer these questions alone or with your supervisor.)

How have you, as leader of the group, experienced the meeting?

Have you been able to follow the meeting plan or have you had to make allowance for the length of the participants' stories?

Have they all had a chance to express themselves, even though they may not have been able to tell their story?

How do you feel about the group's atmosphere?

Some helpful readings from *To Love Again*:

To lose, p. 6;

What have you lost? p. 7;

Small losses and daily annoyances, p. 8;

Shocking losses, p. 8;

The great losses in love, p. 9;

Not only you, but also my dreams, p. 101.

Fostering the hope of resolving our grief

The meeting's theme:

"Will I ever heal?"

Objectives

1. To gain perspective on our grief.

2. To cultivate the hope of healing.

Meeting outline

1 *Opening remarks*

2 *Centering exercise*

See meeting plan on page 20.

3 *Review of the week*

The leader will invite those participants who are interested to talk about their progress and the highlights of their week.

The group members who did not have a chance to tell their story the week before are invited to do so this week.

4   The meeting's theme

The leader will help the group members understand that grief is not an illness, but a natural
response to loss. He or she will emphasize the fact
that they have the resources to learn and to mature
from this experience. The purpose of the group is
to facilitate this process of healing and growth.

The leader will make suggestions and introduce the
creed (see page 19). He or she will hand out copies
of the creed and will read it aloud, or ask someone
to read it aloud.

5   Exchange and sharing

Then the leader will ask participants:

"How do you respond to the affirmations of the
creed?"

"What do you find most striking?"

"Are there affirmations that you find surprising?"

"What do you do to facilitate your grieving process?"

If there is time, the leader can explain briefly the
various stages of the grieving process (see "Brief
description" on page 33).

6   Health break

7   Adjournment of the meeting

Make any announcements concerning the group.

Suggest reading material.

Emphasize that it is very valuable for members to record important events, thoughts, emotions, quotes and so on in their journals.

8 *Prayer or energy chain*

To know if you have met the objectives of the meeting, ask yourself the following questions.

(Answer these questions alone or with your supervisor.)

How have you, as leader of the group, experienced the meeting?

Do you feel that all participants had a chance to tell their story?

Are some members taking too much time?

Are some members too quiet?

Some helpful readings from *To Love Again*:

Joy and losses, the fabric of daily life, p. 35;

My freedom will come from what I fear the most, p. 63;

The ups and downs of the healing process, p. 72;

Healing, p. 94;

My boat is drifting, p. 105.

Coming to terms with our resistance to the loss and expressing our sadness

The meeting's theme:

> "Why do I feel worse than before?"

Objectives

1. Discovering and dealing with resistance that may complicate the grieving process.

2. Expressing sadness.

Meeting outline

1 *Opening remarks*

2 *Centering exercise*

See the meeting plan on page 20.

3 *Reading of the creed*

4 *Review of the week*

Those who want to can read from their journal. Others may wish to tell their fellow members about their progress and the highlights of the week.

5 Presenting the meeting's theme

Based on the experiences shared by the participants, the leader can point out that at this stage in their grief they may feel worse than when they began. In fact, this is a sign of growth, though some may disagree. What they consider a setback is actually a period of thaw before a renewal takes place.

Briefly describe common ways people resist loss and the stages of shock and denial (see page 33).

Warn them against the temptation to leave the group at this point. Remind them that everyone learns at a different pace and that comparing oneself to others serves no purpose.

6 Exchange and sharing

With the help of a few questions, the leader will ask the members to express what was just said:

"Do you allow yourself to cry? When? With whom?"

"Are you afraid of bothering others, especially the members of your family who do not want to hear about grief or see you cry?"

"What would help you express your sadness?"

"Do you allow yourself to become like a child and to let your emotions show?"

"Are you afraid of forgetting your loved one if you let your emotions out?"

Assist the members in understanding that by expressing their emotions they will speed up their

Our reluctance to enter into grief and our attempts to resist it allow us time to become gradually aware of our loss. It also gives us time to develop the inner resources which will enable us to look at the whole picture. When this resistance begins to weaken after a few weeks, we will feel our sadness intensely and may even experience depression. It is normal, then, to feel worse at this time.

Often the state of shock that accompanies a loss may be followed by a state of lethargy, or by inner turmoil and over-activity. At times, we believe that we see, hear, and even touch the deceased.

Denial will manifest itself in a desire to forget what happened or an inability to express emotions. People in this state will say things like: "It's like a nightmare and I can't wait to wake up"; "I can't believe it"; "I know it happened, but it's as if I am not really aware of it"; "It's as if I have been hit on the head with a hammer and I am waiting for the pain to start"; "I stay away from funeral parlours, cemeteries, hospitals or anything that reminds me of death"; "I don't want to talk about it in the house"; "I wish I could cry, but I can t."

Sadness can manifest itself through chronic fatigue, a short attention span, loss of motivation to work, disinterest, loss of appetite, sleeplessness or tearfulness.

grieving process. They will then be able to let their loved ones go, without having to forget them.

7 Health break

8 Adjournment of the meeting

If the members of the group seem to be drawing close to one another, invite them to ask for help from one another (baby-sitting, housekeeping and so forth).

Assign them a task for the week: they are to take a walk in nature during which they can reminisce and get in touch with their bodies.

Remind them of the benefits of keeping a journal.

9 Prayer or energy chain

To know if you have met the objectives of the meeting, ask yourself the following questions.

(Answer these questions alone or with your supervisor.)

How have you, as leader of the group, experienced the personal relaxation period?

How much time do you spend speaking in comparison to the participants?

Make sure that your behaviour does not encourage participants to be passive. Do they perceive you as a teacher?

Some helpful readings from *To Love Again*:

First stage: shock, p. 37;

Second stage: denial, pp. 38-39.;

Forms of denial, pp. 40-41;

The heart that refuses to suffer, pp. 42-43;

The full realization of the loss; the great lament, p. 48;

The emotional merry-go-round, p. 49;

Life-giving emptiness, p. 13;

I am drowning, p. 60;

Give yourself the right to suffer, p. 64;

I thought I was invincible, p. 65.

Becoming aware of our anger and expressing it

The meeting's theme:

"I resent her; I resent him."

Objective

To become aware of our anger during this time of grief, and of the importance of expressing it in a healthy and direct manner.

Meeting outline

1 *Opening remarks*

2 *Centering exercise*

3 *Reading of the creed*

4 *Review of the week*

Members who wish to can read passages from their journal or talk about their experience of grief during the week.

5 *Introduction of the theme*

The leader will explain the purpose of anger in the grieving process.

People who are grieving may feel angry. Typically this anger will not be directed at the person who is gone. Nonetheless, feeling abandoned by a loved one, feeling hurt and aggressive is perfectly legitimate. Very few people can say: "I resent you for abandoning me, for creating a great void within me, for forcing me to take on unexpected responsibilities." Most people express their feelings of anger by asking questions: "Why did you leave so soon?"; "Why did you leave when I needed you the most?"; "Why did God take you away from me?"

They often direct their anger at others. They want to find someone to blame; perhaps the nursing staff who did a poor job, or members of the family who were entrusted with the care of the person—they should have called the doctor sooner, and so forth.

Such accusations can create family conflicts. It is understandable that the reading of the will sometimes turns into a confrontation.

They can also direct their anger at God: "Why did you take my child? I will stop praying or going to church."

Sometimes they will turn this anger in upon themselves, and end up feeling guilty.

6 Exchange and sharing

The leader will ask questions to elicit reactions to the theme that was just presented:

"Do you recognize yourself in the above descriptions?"

"How do you react to the void created by this absence?"

"Is there friction with your relatives as a result of this death?"

7   *Health break*

8   *Adjournment of the meeting*

This would be a good time to quickly assess the meetings and the leadership style. You could ask group members:

"Are you satisfied?"

"Do you have suggestions to make?"

Remind them of the importance of keeping a journal.

9   *Prayer Reading*

End the meeting with "A prayer to a silent God." (See page 23 of this manual.)

To know if you have met the objectives of the meeting, ask yourself the following questions.

(Answer these questions alone or with your supervisor.)

Do you feel that the participants understand that anger is a positive energy? How do you know?

If group members have expressed anger, have you been able to welcome it? If not, how could you learn to accept your own inner anger?

Did all the members have the opportunity to express themselves? How could you encourage the quiet ones to speak without forcing them?

Do you experience specific problems of leadership? Can your supervisor help you to overcome them?

Some helpful readings from *To Love Again*:

> *Anger*, p. 47;
> *The temptation of suicide*, p. 90;
> *You have the right to get angry*, p. 112.

Expressing our feelings of guilt and letting them be transformed

The meeting's theme:

"It's my fault."

Objective

Expressing feelings of guilt and, if possible, transforming obsessional guilt into existential guilt.

Meeting outline

1 *Opening remarks*

2 *Centering exercise*

3 *Reading of the creed*

4 *Review of the week*

The members will describe their experience during the week. The leader will be especially attentive to expressions of anger and aggressiveness as a result of last week's topic.

5 Introduction of the theme

The leader can use some examples given by the participants to introduce this stage of guilt in the grieving process.

A word on obsessional guilt.

Losing a loved one often causes not only sadness but guilt. These attacks of guilt manifest themselves in an accusing inner voice. The bereaved will be inclined to blame themselves: "Shouldn't I have spoken to him before he left?"; "I should have told her that I loved her more often"; "I should have made up before he died"; "I should have taken care of her more"; "I was stupid to act the way I did."

People who are grieving have a tendency to compare themselves to others: "See how courageous she is?; she isn't a wimp like me"; "If I had been prepared like my husband told me, it wouldn't have happened."

This kind of inner dialogue can be exhausting. It drains us of our energy and, in the end, we accuse ourselves of being self-accusatory! It can also result in a state of moderate depression.

Obsessional guilt often stems from not having expressed our feelings to our loved one. The unspoken then turns against us to burden us. Sometimes we are so tired as a result of the care we provided through a long illness that we cannot bear the pain of grief. Nervous chills invade our body with anxious twitches.

Existential guilt, on the other hand, comes as a result of accepting our human limitations, our weaknesses, our faults and our tendency to make mistakes.

The best way to eliminate obsessional guilt is to recognize that we are needy, powerless and weak in the face of extreme sorrow. In a word, we must accept the limits of our humanity.

6 Exchange and sharing

The leader will ask questions to elicit a response from the participants to what was just said:

"Do you recognize yourself in the above descriptions?"

"If so, what do you do with these voices?"

"Do you recognize in these voices comments made by your parents?"

To assist the members in accepting existential guilt, the leader can suggest that they tell themselves: "I am doing my best"; "This is the best that I could do in this situation"; "I accept feeling powerless in the face of this loss."

When they have tried this in their minds, the leader can ask them:

How do you feel when you hear these words?

The leader will help them to discover that the best way to eliminate guilt is to accept our human limitations.

7 Health break

8 Adjournment of the meeting

Invite members who feel ready to write a letter to the one who has left them. This is an excellent way to express what they could not say, or did not have time to say, before they were separated. They can write this letter in their journal while looking at a photograph of the loved one and burning a candle.

9 Prayer or energy chain

To know if you have met the objectives of the meeting, ask yourself the following questions.

> (Answer these questions alone or with your supervisor.)
>
> How would you assess the atmosphere in the group?
>
> Do you think that letting participants express themselves is more important than following the meeting plan?
>
> How would you know that participants understand the nature of healthy feelings of guilt?

Some helpful readings from *To Love Again*:

> *Depression and guilt*, p. 46;
>
> *The fear of going crazy with sadness*, p. 61;
>
> *The temptation of suicide*, p. 90;
>
> *You have the right to get angry*, p. 112.

Taking care of ourselves during the grieving process

The meeting's theme:

> "I know how to take care of myself."

Objective

> To find ways to take care of ourselves while experiencing the grieving process.

Meeting outline

1 *Opening remarks*

2 *Centering exercise*

3 *Reading of the creed*

4 *Review of the week*

5 *Introduction of the theme*

> The leader explains that the grieving process requires a lot of energy. For a certain period, the bereaved may be severely stressed out. They must learn to take care of themselves, to reduce their level of stress and to give themselves every opportunity to resolve their grief.
>
> Here are some ways to do this:

How to take care of yourself during the grieving process
(This list can be photocopied and handed out to participants.)

- Eat regularly and sleep well.
- Resolve problems of insomnia.
- Take breaks from grieving (periods of leisure and relaxation, to be in better shape to grieve).
- Follow your daily routine as much as possible, and include periods of relaxation.
- Take advantage of moments of intense emotion to express these feelings (e.g., while watching a television program, listening to moving music or reading a book.)
- Give yourself times of solitude to assimilate your grief.
- Find a person who is able to listen well.
- Tell yourself that grief will pass and that your life will begin again.
- Avoid making important decisions or spending time with people who drain your energy; avoid excessive fatigue and dangerous situations (violent sports, excessive speed and so on).
- Always choose relaxation, leisure, someone's hand or a massage over tranquilizers and alcohol.
- Surround yourself with other people or living things (plants, animals).
- Learn to control accusing inner voices by answering them through singing or dancing.
- Recite love litanies (my mother loves me, Jim loves me, my dog loves me, the sun loves me, nature loves me, my friends love me). (See "Love and friendship litanies" in *To Love Again*, p. 71.)
- Realize that it is possible to think less often of the lost one, without forgetting that person.
- Be encouraged by the progress you have made.
- Accept temporary relapses and setbacks—these are often accompanied by a new impetus towards health.
- Take time to really heal; avoid seeking comfort in false well-being, and avoid getting really tired.
- Regain your spiritual resources (prayers from childhood, places of meditation).
- Regain your spiritual and religious vision of life after death.

6   Exchange and sharing

Once the leader has read the list, or asked a member to read it, he will ask the participants:

"Do you know other ways of taking care of yourself?"

"In what ways could you take care of yourself during the coming week?"

"What might prevent you from following these suggestions?"

7   Health break

8   Adjournment of the meeting

Ask members to jot down ways of taking care of themselves that are suitable for them.

Invite them to make a commitment to a fellow participant that they will discuss how they have implemented these suggestions.

9   Prayer or energy chain

To know if you have met the objectives of the meeting, ask yourself the following questions.

(Answer these questions alone or with your supervisor.)

Did all members commit to choosing a specific and verifiable way to incorporate well-being in their daily lives?

If not, how would you assess the resistance of the member or members to meeting this objective?

Some helpful readings from *To Love Again*:

Open the dialogue with your inner child, p. 70;

Shedding light on our human relationships

The meeting's theme:

"We don't talk anymore"

Objective

Distinguishing between the people who contribute to resolving your grief and those who do not.

Meeting outline

1 *Opening remarks*

2 *Centering exercise*

3 *Reading of the creed*

4 *Review of the week*

Give participants a moment to tell the member whom they had chosen last week, how they took care of themselves during the past few days.

5 *Introduction of the theme*

The leader will remind participants of how difficult relationships can be in times of grief.

Grief is a stressful situation. It is often a time of tension in your relationships.

Among members of a family it is often understood that no one should mention the dead person, to avoid causing pain. This silence can become oppressive for everyone.

A couple may have lost a child, but the grandparents avoid the subject.

The bereaved may have expected more support from family members, but did not receive it. The family members may be just too sad, unable to talk about it or to console someone else.

The children may feel abandoned. Their parents do not talk about the deceased person and are unable to give them attention or affection.

When a member of a family passes away, other members may begin making underhanded accusations: "If they had cared for him more…"; "If you had not caused him so much pain…"; "Did you see her at the funeral service? She acted as if she were the only one in pain."

Teenagers may withdraw for fear of having to take the place of a lost parent. Alternatively, children will want to take the place of the deceased in their other parent's life.

There is often disagreement and anger over the will.

6 Exchange and sharing

The leader will ask members about difficult relationships in their families:

"Do you recognize yourself in the above situations?"

"Do you experience tension with the people near you?"

"Have you found ways of resolving these conflicts?"

"Who has helped you during your process of grieving?"

7 Health break

8 Adjournment of the meeting

Make any announcements regarding the group.

Inform participants of resources (books, conferences, workshops).

Emphasize that it is very helpful for each person to write in their journal about their thoughts and feelings, or events in their daily life.

9 Prayer or energy chain

To know if you have met the objectives of the meeting, ask yourself the following questions.

(Answer these questions alone or with your supervisor.)

How did members respond to your questions? Could they relate to the situations that you presented?

Were members able to identify helpful and "toxic" people? Did they suggest positive ways of handling their relationships?

Some helpful readings from *To Love Again*:

The forsaken friend, p. 82;

Do not hesitate to ask for help, p. 83;

Cultivate life around you, p. 84;

The sight of other people's happiness pains me, p. 88;

I have sensitive skin, p. 116;

Caution: Do not rush your healing process, p. 100.

Becoming pro-active and resolving unfinished business

The meeting's theme:

> "I still have much to do."

Objective

To take concrete action to resolve "unfinished business" arising from grief.

Meeting outline

1 *Opening remarks*

2 *Centering exercise*

3 *Reading of the creed*

4 *Review of the week*

Invite participants to share ways in which they were able to improve their relationships during the past week.

5 *Introduction of the theme*

The leader will explain that making external gestures to reflect the work that has been accomplished "inside" is very important in the emotional progress of grief. He or she will suggest ways to accelerate the grieving process:

- Finish dialogues with the lost one and give form to things unspoken through visits to the cemetery, letters to the deceased and so on.

- Fulfil promises that you made to the deceased. If fulfilling a particular promises is impossible, replace this by another meaningful one.

- Perform cultural rituals for the remains of the person (place a tombstone, bury the ashes, offer a commemorative mass, and so on), if these have not been done.

- If possible, display only one photograph of the deceased person and place the others in an album. Give away the belongings of the deceased gradually.

- Resolve issues connected with the estate and conditions of the will.

6 Exchange and sharing

Here are some questions to begin the exchange between members:

"What tasks are still to be performed?"

"What difficulties do you experience in performing these tasks?"

"Who could help you accomplish these tasks?"

7 Health break

8 Adjournment of the meeting

Invite participants to write in their journal things relating to their loss that still remain unsaid or undone.

Encourage them to take care of themselves and of their health.

9 Prayer or energy chain

To know if you have met the objectives of the meeting, ask yourself the following questions.

(Answer these questions alone or with your supervisor.)

Is the atmosphere in the group still positive?

How did the meeting go?

Some helpful readings from *To Love Again*:

Letting go of the last hope, p. 99;

Classified ad, p. 108;

Give yourself the right to go through it, p. 110;

When sadness has a hold on you, p. 117;

From isolation to solitude, p. 135;

From the desert to the inner oasis, p. 136.

Discovering a meaning to our loss

The meeting's theme:

"Why did this happen to me?"

Objective

To reflect on the significance of this loss in your life.

Meeting outline

1 *Opening remarks*

2 *Centering exercise*

3 *Reading of the creed*

4 *Review of the week*

5 *Introduction of the theme*

The leader will explain how important it is to reflect on the meaning of this loss even though we have no answers yet. The answer will grow unconsciously and will surface gradually.

The leader can point out that many people discover resources in themselves that they did not suspect, as a result of hardship. They know themselves and in others, they are more compassionate towards the suffering of others, they find a new direction in their work or a new mission in life, and so on.

6   Exchange and sharing

To assist group members in finding meaning to their loss, the leader can ask the same questions in different ways. For example:

"What new resources have you discovered in yourself since the death of your loved one?"

"What significance will this loss assume in your life?"

"What changes do you expect from having a deeper knowledge of yourself, and from choosing a new direction in life?"

"Have your values changed?"

"What new skills are you learning in this difficult period?"

7   Health break

8   Adjournment of the meeting

Remind the participants that there are only two meetings left.

Encourage them to find meaning in their loss and to write about it in their journal.

9 Prayer or energy chain

To know if you have met the objectives of the meeting, ask yourself the following questions.

(Answer these questions alone or with your supervisor.)

Do you feel that participants have understood the questions about the "meaning of the loss?"

Are some participants beginning to find meaning in their experience?

Did you notice some resistance to these questions by the participants? Do you feel that they are ready to go on from this stage?

Some helpful readings from *To Love Again:*

Growing, p. 128;

Because you have loved you are not the same, p. 129;

I was carrying an unknown treasure, p. 131;

Who invented the word failure?, p. 139;

It is time to change, p. 141;

You can now face the inevitable losses of your life, p. 148;

I am proud of myself, p. 143.

Forgiving ourselves and the person we have lost

The meeting's theme:

Forgiveness

Objective

Forgiving the person you have lost, forgiving yourself, and asking for forgiveness.

Meeting outline

1   *Opening remarks*

2   *Centering exercise*

3   *Reading of the creed*

4   *Review of the week*

Participants who wish can share their progress in finding meaning to their loss or simply in their grieving process.

5   *Introduction of the theme*

The leader will explain the importance of forgiveness and its impact. By granting forgiveness, we can stop feeling angry towards our loved one. By asking for forgiveness, we alleviate our feelings of guilt. (See "Forgiving" on page 38).

6 Exchange and sharing

During this meeting, it is very beneficial to take a moment of silence to invite participants to place themselves mentally face to face with their loved one, and then to forgive them for their shortcomings and for having departed.

Participants can then share their experience of this gesture of forgiveness.

In a second period of silence, participants can ask for forgiveness for their own shortcomings.

Remind participants that they do not have to forgive immediately. They must proceed at their own pace. Most importantly, they must know where they are in relation to this stage. They may still feel too much sadness and anger to forgive. Being aware of their own feelings is, in itself, an important step.

Questions to ask participants:

"What happened when you began to grant forgiveness?"

"Do you find it easier to grant forgiveness than to ask forgiveness?"

What else might you do to assist participants in experiencing this stage?

7 Health break

8 Adjournment of the meeting

- Remind participants that there is only one meeting left. Suggest that they organize a celebration and a pot-luck dinner.

- Invite them to write in their journal what the group has done for them up to this point, and how they plan to continue their grieving process.

- If you know of another group that is starting, invite them to join it to continue the process of resolving their grief.

- Suggest other resources (e.g., going through the process in another group or seeing a counsellor or a therapist).

- Ask participants if they are ready for the ritual of legacy.

Are you ready to claim your legacy?

Granting and receiving forgiveness is essential before performing the ritual of legacy. (See "Taking possession of your legacy" on pp. 154-155 of *To love again*.)

If one or two members of the group are ready to perform this ritual, ask them to:

1. Find objects symbolizing the qualities of their loved one that they would like to possess; and
2. Name these qualities (see p. 154 of *To Love Again*).

   If no one is ready to perform the ritual of legacy, ask members to:

1. Bring an object that symbolizes the spiritual wealth of the deceased; and
2. Bring an object that represents the progress that they have made in their grieving process.

The ritual of "removing from the pedestal."

It is no longer a question of reclaiming what we have invested in the person whom we have lost, but of freeing ourselves from the yoke that we feel (the burden of suffering, or perhaps a feeling of responsibility for the other person's drinking problem, and so on.)

Ask the participants to:
1. Think about those responsibilities that they have taken on, and that are not theirs; and
2. Write them down or draw an image of them.
   These notes and drawings will be burned at the last meeting.

9 Prayer or energy chain

The leader may have noticed group members who are ready to lead a support group. Take them aside and invite them to do so.

To know if you have met the objectives of the meeting, ask yourself the following questions.

(Answer these questions alone or with your supervisor.)

Were you able to complete all of the tasks related to this meeting?

Do participants understand the importance of forgiving the person who has left them?

How have they reacted to the ritual of legacy? Did some participants express jealousy?

Some helpful readings from *To Love Again*:

My beloved, I could not see your flaws, p. 73;

Forgiving the other person, p. 145;

Forgiving him, forgiving her, p. 146;

Forgiving myself, p. 144.

Twelfth meeting

Claiming our legacy

The meeting's theme:

"I take back what I loaned you"

Objective

Claiming for ourselves what we have loved in the other person.

Meeting outline

1 *Opening remarks*

2 *Centering exercise*

3 *Reading of the creed*

4 *Review of the week*

Participants can share with one another what the group has given to them.

5 *Introduction of the theme*

If members are ready to perform the ritual of legacy, the leader can review its meaning and the procedure to follow. (See "Taking possession of your legacy" on pp. 154-155 of *To Love Again*.)

• The leader can follow the ritual described in *To Love Again*.

- The leader can invite participants to explain the symbolism of their objects and to make a gesture indicating that they are claiming them.

6 Exchange and sharing

The leader can invite participants to perform a ritual of unburdening. The members who are ready and have prepared their notes or drawing are invited to:

1. Tell the group what responsibility they are rejecting; and

2. Burn their note or drawing.

At the end of the ritual the leader will officially announce that those who have performed these rituals have completed their process of grieving. (See "Acknowledging the end of grief and celebrating it" on p. 39.)

The leader will emphasize to the ones who do not perform any of the above rituals the importance of respecting themselves and their own time-frame. The leader can also ask the members who do not perform the rituals to share their thoughts, and point out that witnessing the ritual usually brings hope to those who are not quite ready to perform it.

7 Adjournment of the final meeting

By organizing a celebration participants will have an opportunity to thank each other and to share a meal.

If they prefer to go to a restaurant, make sure that they do not leave before having said good-bye to one another.

To know if you have met the objectives of this meeting, and of the series as a whole, ask yourself the following questions.

(Answer these questions alone or with your supervisor.)

What have you learned about yourself and about others?

Would you like to experience this over again?

Do you feel that some members may be ready to lead a group?

Take time to congratulate yourself for the wonderful work that you have accomplished.

Some helpful readings from *To Love Again*:

Seventh stage: claiming the legacy, p. 55;

Growing a garden in foreign ground, p. 149;

Reaping what you have sown during the relationship, p. 151;

Janet takes back what belongs to her, pp. 152-153;

Taking possession of your legacy, pp. 154-155;

You will be filled with a new presence, p. 160;

I never thought I could thank you and congratulate myself, pp. 164-165.

Bibliography

Caine, Lynn. *Being a Widow*. New York: Viking Penguin Books, 1990.

Deits, Bob. *Life after Loss: A Personal Guide to Dealing with Death, Divorce, Job Change and Relocation*. Rev. ed., Tucson, Arizona: Fisher Books, 1992.

Grollman, Earl, ed. *Concerning Death: A Practical Guide for the Living*. Boston: Beacon Press, 1974.

Grollman, Earl. *Living When a Loved One Has Died*. Boston: Beacon Press, 1977.

Kavanaugh, Robert. *Facing Death*. New York: Viking Penguin Books, 1972.

Monbourquette, Jean. *To Love Again*. Ottawa: Novalis, 1993.

Sarnoff, Harriet Shiff. *The Bereaved Parent*. New York: Viking Penguin Books, 1978.

Spiegel, Yorick. *The Grief Process: Analysis and Counseling*. Trans. Elsbeth Duke, Nashville: Abingdon, 1977.

Tatelbaum, Judy. *The Courage to Grieve: Creative Living, Recovery and Growth Through Grief*. New York: Harper Collins, 1984.

Appendix 1

Advice for surviving and growing after the suicide of a loved one

1. Even though it may be impossible to believe right now, you will survive this suicide and even grow from the experience.

2. At the beginning, you must learn to live one moment, one hour, one day at a time.

3. Find one person, or a few people, who can listen to you when you need to unburden yourself.

4. Try not to torment your heart and mind with questions. Be still, and one day soon the answers will come unexpectedly.

5. At times, you will feel overwhelmed by emotions. These emotions are normal in your situation. Remember that they are temporary.

6. Feeling afraid and vulnerable is natural.

7. Anger, guilt and confusion are normal emotions in your situation. You are not going crazy, only grieving deeply.

8. Give yourself the right to feel guilty towards the person who committed suicide. Also, allow yourself to feel angry towards that person.

9. Feeling angry with the world and with God is also a normal response. Give yourself permis-

sion to feel angry and find positive ways to express this emotion. It will pass.

10. You have the right to feel guilty for your actions or inactions, for what you said and did not say. Gradually guilt will turn into regret, and then into helplessness in the face of this suicide.

11. Begin to understand the reasons that caused your loved one to find a solution in suicide. Tell yourself that it was their decision. Give yourself time to come to terms with their decision.

12. Some people who are close to a person who commits suicide may themselves develop suicidal thoughts. However, having these thoughts does not mean that you must act on them.

13. Crying is the most natural way to express sadness, and to release it.

14. Give yourself time to heal.

15.   Remember that the decision to commit suicide was not yours. Accept your helplessness in being unable to influence your loved one.

16. Emotions related to grief come in waves. They roll on the shore, recede and then return again.

17.   Put off making important decisions. Avoid taking risks.

18. Give yourself the opportunity to receive professional help, if necessary. Joining a support group can be helpful. Often strangers can be

more helpful than relatives and friends, who may also be grieving.

19. Be patient with yourself, and with others who do not always understand what you are experiencing.

20. Define your limitations and learn to refuse to take on more work than you can easily manage.

21. Rely on your faith and seek spiritual solutions.

22. Feeling depressed, tired or physically ill is normal.

23. Remember, you are allowed to take a break from your grief to enjoy yourself and play.

24. Let go of all your questions, your overwhelming emotions and remorse. Gradually, the memory of the one you have lost will become more bearable.

25. As a result of a trial like this you will not be the same. You will have lived more deeply and fully; you will have matured.

26. Day by day you will discover meaning in this tragedy. Ask yourself, What is the meaning of this experience? What is this painful situation teaching you?

Appendix 2

Advice on grieving the loss of a child

Of all the experiences of grief, the most painful one is undoubtedly the death of a child as a result of an accident, an illness, a miscarriage or even an abortion.

Here are some points to look for in these situations.

1. The death of a child is such a deep cause of grief because parents usually identify strongly with their children. They see in them a continuation of themselves and their future. Since parents are responsible for the development and safety of their children, they may feel that their child's death means that they have failed. They experience tremendous guilt.

2. It is not unusual for parents who have lost a child to accuse each other of being responsible for the death. Such accusations are not always explicit; they can be expressed through impatience and irritability toward the "guilty party".

3. The death of a child is often accompanied by a breakdown of communication between parents. Instead of being present to one another, they will ask each other to stop crying, to stop talking about the child because it will bring not him or her back.

This form of rejection causes the partners to close off and to stop communicating.

4. Parents who have lost a child do not always grieve at the same pace. They will, in turn, experience periods of acute pain followed by remissions. Sometimes, when one partner overcomes a difficult moment, he or she may feel dragged down again by the other's latest bout of depression. To avoid painful situations, partners tend to avoid one another.

5. Partners must realize that they are unique and that they will experience grief differently. One will express his or her emotions openly, while the other may repress them. One will lose himself or herself in work, while the other will be constantly tired. One will want to reminisce, while the other will want to forget. Partners will need much understanding and tolerance to let each other experience grief in their own way without feeling threatened.

6. The intensity of grief will vary according to the relationship between the parent and the child, and according to the parent's aspirations and expectations. Thus the emotional intensity of grief experienced by one partner may seem disproportionate to the other partner.

7. The death of a child can also affect a couple's sexuality. One may experience an increase in his or her sexual drive, while the other may feel a decrease. This upheaval can last up to two years after the death of the child. This is why partners must engage in an open dialogue about their sexual

feelings. They may even need professional counselling.

8. The changes caused by the experience of grief may become a source of discomfort and even conflict between the partners. One may become confused and unable to adapt to the rapid changes of the other.

9. To live through the death of a child, couples may require professional help.

MARQUIS

PRINTED BY THE WORKERS OF
IMPRIMERIE D'ÉDITION MARQUIS
IN AUGUST 1994
MONTMAGNY (QUÉBEC)